EXTRAORDINARY
Short Story Writing

by Steven Otfinoski

Franklin Watts®

A Division of Scholastic Inc.
New York • Toronto • London • Auckland • Sydney
Mexico City • New Delhi • Hong Kong
• Danbury, Connecticut

EXTRAORDINARY SHORT STORY WRITING

ASSIGNMENT:

So, you have been assigned to write a short story. Each state in the country has its own educational curriculum plan for you and other students around your state. These plans are called educational standards. From **California** to **New York**, from **Minnesota** to **Texas**, the standards call for students to tackle a variety of short story projects. In **California**, for instance, ninth and tenth graders are expected to write biographical or auto-biographical narratives or short stories that describe the sights, sounds, and smells of a scene. **Massachusetts** wants eighth graders to write stories with well-developed characters, settings, and dialogue. Even if it's not spelled out in your state's standards, writing short stories gives you a chance to develop skills that will pay off in your other writing assignments.

HOW-TO MINI-GUIDES

THE BACK MATTER

Heads Up!

How To Use This Book

There are lots of extras in this book aimed at helping you with writing your short story.

BRAIN JAM

Brain Jams offer activities to get you thinking creatively and give you a chance to hone your skills.

STORY JUMP START

Story Jump Starts provide that sometimes necessary extra push to get you going on your own story.

TIP FILE

Tip Files offer up all sorts of helpful suggestions and hints on getting the project done.

RESOURCES

This icon will lead you to more information.

ORDINARY   EXTRAORDINARY

Throughout the book you will see the ordinary and the extraordinary side by side. With revisions and some thought, these comparisons show you what you can accomplish.

Photographs © 2005: AP/Wide World Photos: 46 (Jim McKnight), 14 (Stuart Ramson), 90 (Eric Risberg); Corbis Images/Bettmann: 79; Corbis Sygma/Sophie Bassouls: 27; Getty Images/Kevin Winter: 102; Library of Congress: 11, 22; Noel Sturgeon: 102.

Cover Design: Marie O'Neill
Page design: Simon Says Design!
Cover and interior illustration by Kevin Pope.

Library of Congress Cataloging-in-Publication Data

Otfinoski, Steven.
  Extraordinary short story writing / Steven Otfinoski.
    p. cm. — (F. W. Prep)
  Includes bibliographical references and index.
  ISBN 0-531-16760-7 (lib. bdg.)   0-531-17578-2 (pbk.)
  1. Short story—Authorship. I. Title. II. Series. III. Series: F. W. Prep
  PN3373.O84 2005
  808.3'1—dc22
                                                        2005006650

144- 9408

SHORT STORY

So see, you're not alone. Thousands of other students are tackling the same types of assignments this year. How do you make your assignment catch your teacher's attention? How do you give your project a twist that makes it distinct from all the others? In a word, how do you make it EXTRAORDINARY?

Part of making any project EXTRAORDINARY—whether it's a short story, essay, or research project—is knowing what is expected of you and surpassing those expectations. Regard these assignments as opportunities for you to develop and express your own creative ideas—while developing your skills as a writer and storyteller!

And now for the short story report... Biographical narratives are blanketing the West Coast... and hundreds of thousands of well-developed characters are being predicted in Texas...

Check Out Your State's Standards!

One way to stay ahead of the game is to take a look at your state's standards for this year and the years ahead. If you're ready to look into your future, try visiting Developing Educational Standard's site at: **http://www.edstandards.org/Standards.html.** On it, you can find links to the educational departments of every state and even focus on language arts in particular.

For more of a national overview of language arts standards, here's a few of the twelve national educational standards created by the National Council of Teachers of English (NCTE). (For a complete list, visit NCTE's Web site, **http://www.ncte.org.**)

By writing short stories, you demonstrate several key skills mentioned in the standards:

- An extraordinary short story indicates that you know how to use written language to communicate effectively with a range of audiences and for different purposes.

- The creative and logical tools you use while writing an extraordinary short story demonstrates your knowledge of writing strategies and the writing process and that you can use them effectively.

- An extraordinary short story is an example of your knowledge of language structure, language conventions, figurative language, and genre and that you can employ this knowledge to create texts.

"We all have the EXTRAORDINARY coded within us, waiting to be released."

—Jean Houston

Heads Up!

So Here's the Scoop

When teachers grade short stories, they use a number of factors based on educational standards to determine your grade. Here are some.

Characters: Are they believable and well-rounded? Do they hold the readers attention?

Conflict: Is the conflict a strong one? Is it set in an interesting plot?

Organization: Is the language clear? Can the reader follow the story's events without confusion?

Dialogue: Does the dialogue sound like real conversation? Does it move the action forward?

Setting: Is it appropriate to the plot and characters? Do descriptive details make it identifiable and real for the reader?

Descriptive detail: Are they well thought out and well written? Do they help the reader visualize what is happening?

Theme(s): A theme is an idea or concept that is developed in a short story. Do the theme or themes naturally come out of the conflict and characters? Does it give the reader something to think about after finishing the story?

What's a Short Story Anyway?

Although stories have been told since the dawn of humankind, the first written stories only appeared about 5,000 years ago in ancient Egypt (that's 3000 BCE [before the common era], if you didn't know). There were many great stories written after that, including such famous story collections as *The Arabian Nights,* and *The Canterbury Tales* by the English author **Geoffrey Chaucer**. However, the modern short story didn't come into its own until quite recently, in the nineteenth century.

Some of the first writers to take the short story seriously were such American authors as **Washington Irving, Nathaniel Hawthorne,** and **Edgar Allan Poe**. They all had a keen interest in the grotesque and the supernatural. Poe, for example, wrote some of the scariest and creepiest stories ever published. He also was the creator of the modern detective story. But he was also an important literary critic who championed the short story and wrote about what he thought it should be.

WORD COUNT REALITY CHECK

1,197 words,
1,198 words,
1,199 words,
2,000 words.
Done!

"A short story must have a single mood and every sentence must build towards it."

—Edgar Allan Poe
(1809-1849)

Poe defined a short story as a brief work of fiction that can be read from start to finish in one sitting. Later critics and writers have been more exact, saying a short story should be between about 2,000 and 8,000 words. A longer work of fiction is called a novella. Longer still, and it's a novel.

You can find the word count for a story using the word count tool in your word processing program.

***Short* Short Story**	☞	*up to 2,000 words*
Short Story	☞	*2,000–8,000 words*
Novella	☞	*8,000–40,000 words*
Novel	☞	*50,000 words and up*

Elements of the Short Story

(and the Novel, too)

Conflict

All fiction is built around conflict. A conflict is a struggle between two forces. In a story or novel, the conflict is usually between a central character whom we call the **protagonist**, or hero, and someone or something else. Here are **three kinds of conflicts** in fiction:

The Protagonist vs. Another Person (Antagonist). The antagonist can be a villain or anyone who stands in the hero's way and must be defeated.

The Protagonist vs. A Force of Nature. This can be a storm, a volcano, an earthquake, a wild animal, or anything else in the natural world that poses a threat or challenge to the protagonist.

The Protagonist vs. Himself or Herself. This is called an inner conflict. The protagonist is pulled in two different directions while trying to make an important decision. It could be a struggle within the hero of good against evil.

Often, a good way to define something is to show what it's not. A novel and short story are both works of fiction—one short and one long. But there are some other important differences. A novel has one central conflict to relate through its plot, or its series of events. There may also be several smaller conflicts told in side stories that branch off from the main one. The short story can't afford to have any subplots or conflicts, because it doesn't have the space to develop them. It has one conflict that it follows it through to the end.

Setting

The setting is the place and time in which a story takes place. The setting may be varied in a novel. There may be many places in which the action takes place, and the time covered may be weeks, months, or even years.

A short story, by its very nature, has a much more limited focus. Its conflict often is set in one central place and happens over a brief period of time. But there are plenty of stories that don't conform to this rule, especially in terms of time.

For example, Poe's story **"The Cask of Amontillado"** takes place one night during a carnival in Italy. The central character exacts a terrible revenge on his friend by entombing him behind a wall in his basement. But the main character who is telling the story is recalling the awful act fifty years later and is haunted by guilt—an inner conflict.

Voice

Everyone has a different and unique voice, or way of talking, whether it's funny, serious, insincere, or just plain odd. Characters need to have individual voices, too. Sometimes the voice belongs to the person telling the story in the first person. Other times, the author's voice reveals how she or he feels about the story and the characters in it. One voice will often dominate and color the story. The individual voices of the characters often comes through in the way they talk with each other, which is called dialogue (see page 16). Voice is one important way a writer reveals his or her attitude toward a story's subject.

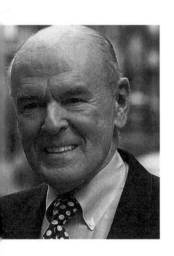

"A story is only as strong as the voices telling it....The only voice a story never needs is the author's. Characters need to speak for themselves in their own distinct voices... Particularly in a short story, every word they speak needs to sound like the speaker and move the story along."

— Richard Peck (1936—)

Characters

Characters are the actors in a story.
Characters don't have to be human. They can be animals or even inanimate objects. In the story **"There Will Come Soft Rains"** by the science fiction writer **Ray Bradbury**, the only character is a house! A novel may have a gallery of many characters. Some are major characters and some minor. A short story, in general, has room for only a few characters. Poe's **"The Cask of Amontillado"** has only two. Having too many characters in a short story would only confuse the reader. There just isn't enough space to develop them.

Point of View

The point of view, or viewpoint, is the perspective from which the story is told. If told in the third person, the story's narrator is objective and not a character in the story. A first-person narrator is a character in the story. It can be the protagonist or another character. A novel can be told from more than one viewpoint. It may be told by several characters, sometimes describing the same events from their own points of view. In a short story, there is only room for one viewpoint. It may be third person or first person. A first-person narrator works well in short stories. He or she gives the story immediacy and draws the reader emotionally into the story. Several of **Edgar Allan Poe**'s best and scariest stories are told in the first person.

Dialogue

Dialogue is the conversation between two or more characters in a story. In a play, all the action is relayed through dialogue. In a story or novel, dialogue alternates with narration in telling the story. Dialogue should not be secondary to what is happening in the story. It should advance the action while at the same time define the characters who are speaking—their dreams, desires, and personalities. A character's voice will often come through in the way he or she talks to other people. Each character's speech in dialogue should have its own rhythm, diction, and vocabulary.

While dialogue in stories gives the impression that real people are talking to each other, they are not. To see what we mean, compare dialogue in a story you read with the actual conversation around your dinner table. Real people don't speak in complete sentences. Conversation often starts and stops and has a way of repeating itself. To put real conversation down in a story would not be very interesting to read. However, story dialogue shouldn't be stilted, unnatural, and full of vocabulary people don't normally use. It should sound as natural as possible.

Mood

The atmosphere or feeling in a work of fiction is its mood. The writer creates the mood through setting, characters, and descriptive details. The mood can be funny, frightening, romantic, or adventurous. While a novel can have many moods, a short story normally has only one mood. To add another mood to it would confuse the reader.

So What's a Short Story?

A short story is a work of fiction, usually between 2,000 and 8,000 words long. A short story has...

Only a few **CHARACTERS** with their own **VOICES** who speak in **DIALOGUE.**

One central **CONFLICT.**

One **VIEWPOINT.**

One **MOOD.**

So now that you know what a short story is, let's start writing one.

School Activities

The local ne...

Personal photo...

conversations

albums

Mu...

Photogra...

Ma...

paintings

Family stori...

18

HUNT AND GATHER

Finding Your Story Idea

Finding Your Story Idea

Every story starts as an idea. Pretty obvious, huh? Maybe, but having a good idea for a story is half the battle of writing a good story.

You might say that all good stories come out of the writer's imagination, but the spark that starts the imagination working can come from almost anywhere. The world is filled with stories waiting to be told and written down. All you have to do is look for them. Let's take a closer look at each story idea source listed below.

Your story can be about...

...something that happened to you.

...something that happened to someone you know.

...something you saw, heard, or read in the media.

...something you just made up out of your imagination.

Get a Box!

As you find images, articles, and other material for your short story, you may want to get a box or a binder to hold your possible inspirations. This way, once you're done hunting and gathering, you can easily review what you've got. Newspaper and magazine articles, advertisements, quotes, favorite books, historical facts are all potential sparks for your great work of fiction. A story idea could come from anywhere.

The "Me" Factor: Turning Your Life into a Story

"Write about what you know!" is the advice many professional writers give to newcomers. And who do you know better than yourself? Lots of writers, especially when they are starting out, focus on their own experiences. They write stories and novels that are autobiographical. They take experiences and people from their lives and turn them into stories.

"That's fine," you might be saying, "but I haven't exactly had a very exciting life up until now. What experience have I had that's exciting enough to make into a story that would interest others?" Maybe more experiences than you think. You may not have lived a life full of adventures, but you've had things happen to you that are worth writing about. These include experiences at school, on the playing field, at home, and on vacation. An experience might be funny, scary, serious, or adventurous.

What's important is that it's yours!

Working in Your Sleep

Keep a notepad by your bed. A great idea may strike while you're waiting to fall asleep or even while you're snoozing. Dreams can be a great source for story ideas. Dreams fade quickly, however. Try keeping your eyes shut when you wake up and focusing on the dream. Then immediately jot down the details on your pad.

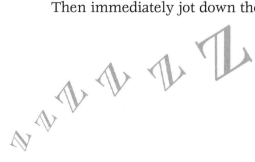

Picture This

Is your mind still a blank? Try this. Take out an old family photo album and look through the pictures. They contain some of the highlights of your life. Seeing these photographs of yourself with family and friends might stimulate your memory and bring back experiences you might have forgotten about. There's sure to be at least one good story told by these pictures.

Whatever experience you decide to write about, don't feel you have to slavishly follow the facts. Your story idea might be good enough to make into a short story with few changes or it might be just the springboard to a story that mixes fiction with fact. The important thing is to grab onto that idea and go with it.

"Did I Tell You About the Time..." Someone Else's Story

It is said that everyone has a book in them. That may or may not be true, but everyone certainly has a story in them. These stories are all around you—as close as your family, friends, and acquaintances.

Older people (parents, grandparents, uncles, and aunts) are a particularly good source for stories, because they have a lot more life experiences to draw on than you do. Next time you're at a family gathering, pull a relative aside and ask that person to tell you about his or her life. You'll probably get a good earful! You're bound to hear some good stories along the way.

Here are some examples:

- a hair-raising experience your granddad had as a young man

- a funny thing that happened to your older brother or sister when he or she went away to college for the first time

- your father's version of his first blind date with your mother (then check out her version of what happened)

- a long-cherished story about how your family came to the United States

You'll probably want to take notes as you listen to these stories. Better yet, tape record or videotape the story if the storyteller doesn't mind. Ask the person if he or she has photographs related to the experience.

These photos might provide some good details and background you can use in your story. Also, make sure you ask for permission to write your story based on the person's experiences. And if there are holes in the story where you don't know what happened, don't hesitate to go back to the source and ask more questions. Your storyteller probably won't mind in the least talking to you again. He or she will most likely be flattered by all the attention!

There you are, my boy.
Do I have a story for you . . .
It begins in the hot sands of the Sahara . . .
And me with only a thimble full of water . . .

One Great Story Deserves Another:
Borrowing from the Media

Every day we're bombarded with stories of all kinds, in the news, in the movies, and on television. You might find the inspiration to write a story based on a scene or character in a movie or a television program you've seen.

The daily newspaper is another great source for story ideas. Try regularly clipping articles that you find interesting, unusual, or just plain bizarre. Keep them in a file folder to look at when you need inspiration or an idea for a new story.

Here are some newsworthy examples:

- A cat returns home after being lost for several months.

- Archeologists discover an ancient temple of a lost civilization in the jungles of Central America.

- An inventor comes up with a new and unusual labor-saving device.

You might find yourself using many of the details from a media story. Or a character, event, or setting just might be the trigger that sets **your imagination in motion.**

Imagination:
The Writer's Secret Weapon

Someone once asked the playwright **Arthur Miller** whom he based the characters on in his play *Death of a Salesman.* Miller replied that he didn't base them on anyone; he made them up. One of the great joys of writing is getting to make things up. A writer's greatest tool is his or her imagination. All stories have bits and pieces of reality in them, but it's the writer's imagination that connects them to create something fresh, new, and extraordinary.

To get your imagination into high gear, you need to spend some time with it. You need some peace and quiet. Impossible, you say?

Here are some things to try that can help put you in touch with your imagination:

- Sit in a park and observe how people interact.

- Take a long walk, outdoors or some other quiet place where you can think and create. Many writers do their best thinking while walking.

- Shut the door to your room, lie down, close your eyes, and listen to a piece of your favorite music.

- Always carry a small notebook and a pen or pencil with you to jot down story ideas.

- Play word games like **Mad Libs®** or **Scrabble®**. Unusual imagery or odd word combinations may trigger a story idea.

"Write down all these slender [story] ideas. It is surprising how often one sentence, jotted in a note-book, leads immediately to a second sentence. A plot can develop as you write notes. Close the notebook and think about it for a few days—and then presto! You're ready to write a short story."

—Patricia Highsmith (1921-1995)

What would happen if...?

Not all story ideas are exciting and fresh, but that's okay. With a little tweaking, they could become some-thing special.

Here's a great technique for turning a tired story idea into an extraordinary one. First, take your idea and summarize it in a sentence. Then, pose a question that begins with the words "What would happen if." Your question should change something about the idea, giving it a new slant or an unexpected twist. Your ques-tion might just spark your imagination, moving it in a direction you hadn't thought about before.

Here are **three** "what would happen if . . . " questions that may have led three fine writers to create truly original stories.

Look at the bottom of the next page to see the title and author. Then, find these stories and read them. They're excellent examples of what a good short story should be.

1 A father is concerned about his sickly baby daughter and wants to make her stronger.

2 A man goes on a hunting trip in the woods with his dog.

3 A writer checks into a hotel for the night.

now...

Three famous writers created
these three imaginative
story ideas.
Can you guess who?

What would happen if...

1 The father is a beekeeper and decides to feed his baby daughter the royal jelly that queen bees feed their offspring?

2 The hunter meets up with a group of strange little men who get him drunk, and he then falls asleep for twenty years?

3 The writer is working on a book about haunted places, and the hotel room he is staying in is supposedly haunted?

A Step-By-Step Guide to Writing a Short Story

To help you understand the steps involved in writing a short story, we're going to come up with our own story idea. Over the next four chapters, we're going to:

- develop an idea from scratch.

- take it through to a finished story.

- choose a situation that you can probably relate to —being a new student in a new school.

Let's put this basic story idea into a sentence:

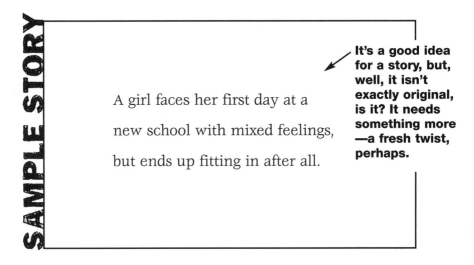

SAMPLE STORY

A girl faces her first day at a new school with mixed feelings, but ends up fitting in after all.

It's a good idea for a story, but, well, it isn't exactly original, is it? It needs something more —a fresh twist, perhaps.

Let's try a **"What would happen if ..."** question and see where it leads us.
In fact, let's try a whole bunch of them.

What would happen
if the new kid at school...

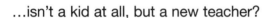

...is an alien from another planet?

...is from Earth, and everyone
else at school is an alien?

...isn't a kid at all, but a new teacher?

All of these ideas present intriguing possibilities for the story. The two ideas having to do with aliens would make for an interesting science fiction story (for more on sci-fi stories, see Chapter 7). But perhaps the most exciting idea of all is the last one. No kid thinks about a new teacher having difficulty adjusting to a new school. If you choose this path for your story idea, you could make some interesting points about how adults can be just as insecure and sensitive as kids are when they find themselves in a new and unfamiliar environment. **Now that's an original story idea!** But let's not stop here while we're on a creative roll. Let's try to refine our idea with another "What would happen if . . ." question about our new teacher!

What would happen if ...

the fact that the central character is a teacher is deliberately kept back from the reader until the very end of the story?

WOW! The reader will think this is a new kid going to school and at the end will be totally surprised to find out that she's a teacher instead. Talk about a surprise ending! Of course, this will take some skillful writing on your part to lead the reader on, keep back the critical information, and still make the story believable. But it could be well worth the effort when the reader comes to the end and is totally floored. That's the kind of effect writers love to have on their readers.

Well, now that we have our idea more fully fleshed out, it's time to take it to the next level and give our story some structure. In **Chapter 2: Outlining Your Story**, we'll plan out your story in detail.

TIME TO GET CREATIVE

Great ideas don't always come as a lightning bolt to the brain. There are ways to enhance your creative powers. So get ready to open your mind, at least a little bit. Choreographer Twyla Tharp helps readers uncover their creative DNA and make it a part of their everyday existence in her book, *The Creative Habit: Learn It and Use It for Life*.

BRAIN JAM:
Finding Your Story Idea

Read about it. Take a newspaper and read the headlines until you find one that grabs your attention. Write the headline on a separate paper in the middle of a circle. Around the circle, like spokes of a wheel, write down any words, images, or phrases that pop into your mind. Once you've exhausted yourself, take a look at the paper.

Mine your own history. Think of something that happened to you that could be a story idea. What is it about this experience would make a good story that would interest other people?

Meet the family. What member of your extended family would you want to interview to get possible story ideas? What experiences has this person had that would make him or her a good source for a story?

Personality tra

Main Character

Minor Charac

Setting

Physical Characte

THE VISION

Outlining Your Story

Outlining Your Story

Every writer approaches the planning of his or her story differently. Some writers like to "wing it" as they go along and let the story idea take them where it will. Other writers plan out their stories meticulously before they write a single word. They like to know exactly where they're going before they get there.

Because you may be new to writing stories, it might be wise to take the second approach. Later, you can decide which way works best for you. For now, an outline will give you a framework and somewhere to start.

That doesn't mean, however, that you have to follow your outline slavishly. The very act of writing, after all, is a journey of discovery. As you get into your story, feel free to alter your outline and improve it. Writing is a creative process that doesn't stop until you've finished your story to your satisfaction.

Before we go any further, let's reexamine the basic elements of a short story and plug in what we already know. This will help us develop our story outline.

"A lot of writers, ... outline in great detail. But the system of ... letting the story grow, seems to me to give you the advantage of letting your characters develop in a way that seems real and natural."

—Tony Hillerman (1925–)

Characters Count: Main Character

Character is the most basic element of all fiction— stories, novellas, novels, and plays too. You can have a short story with a very simple plot, but you can't have a story without a character.

Let's look at the central character in our **sample story**. This character is a teacher about to begin teaching at a new school where she knows no one. Let's draw up a profile of what this character is like. These details will help us write about this person.

CHARACTER PROFILE

SAMPLE STORY

CHARACTER PROFILE: The New Teacher

NAME: Sandy Anders

SEX: Female

AGE: Young, maybe this is only her second teaching job

PHYSICAL CHARACTERISTICS:
medium height, thin, brown hair

PERSONALITY TRAITS:
wants to do well, worries about not being good enough

This is fine for a start. It'll give you an idea of who your character is and what she looks like. You can fill in some of the other details as you write.

Filling Out the Picture: Minor Characters

Most short stories have one or possibly two or three main characters. Our story will have only one— Sandy Anders. The other characters will be minor ones. Sometimes minor characters play an important role in a story. So you need to know more about them. But in our story the minor characters will exist mainly to help develop the action and interact briefly with the main character. A detailed profile of any of them isn't necessary.

Who will these minor characters be? Some of them will definitely be students who appear at the end of the story, when Sandy enters the classroom. There might be a reason to introduce other characters, but let's see how our story develops before we think about that.

Setting:
The Backdrop for Your Story

The role of the setting in a story is determined by the nature of the story and its characters. The setting can exert a powerful influence on both the plot and the characters in some cases. It can set a mood or atmosphere that permeates the entire story. Or it can be merely a backdrop for the action. It is for you, the writer, to determine the setting's role.

Don't forget that the time is as much a part of the story's setting as the place. The time in which a story is set may be determined by the kind of story it is.

- Historical stories will be set in a specific period of the past.

- Most realistic, contemporary stories are set in the present.

- Science fiction and fantasy stories are often set in the future.

We'll look more closely at some of these different kinds of short stories a little later. But now let's get back to our sample story.

- **The setting of our short story:**
  a small city where Sandy's new school is located.

- **The time:** the present.

Plot:
The Main Event

The plot is the backbone of the short story. It's what happens to the main character or what he or she does. In a short story, the plot should not be too complicated. The story may revolve around one central event. **In our case, it is a teacher going to her first day of work at a new school.** The conflict that drives the plot is mostly internal. Sandy fears that she will fail and that the students won't like her. How will she overcome her fears and succeed? Of course, the plot could be quite different if the conflict were changed.

Here are two alternate conflicts that would change the story's plot:

Sandy vs. Another Person On her first day, Sandy Anders is confronted by an unruly student who just won't behave. She is determined to find a way to change the student's attitude without losing her cool—a big challenge for a new teacher on her first day!

Sandy vs. A Force of Nature In the middle of Sandy's first day, the part of town the school is in is struck by a tornado. Sandy is trapped in the building with her students and must keep them safe and calm as the tornado does its damage.

Sum It Up

Once you've got an idea about the plot, it's time to write a summary of your story. **A summary will give you a clearer idea of what your story is about** and will help you develop your outline later.

PLOT SUMMARY

Sandy, a new teacher, wakes up one morning and gets ready to go to her first day at a new school. She is very nervous and doesn't know what to expect. She arrives at school and faces her first class of students and introduces herself to them. For the first time, we realize that Sandy is a teacher and not a student.

Doesn't sound too exciting, does it? Plot summaries often don't. It may need more plot complications. But you can sort that out later. We'll figure out what else it needs as we continue the writing process. For now, we've got a place to start.

The Outline

One way to structure your story is to make an outline. You make outlines in other classes, such as history or science. You can make an outline of a short story, too. Some writers don't like the structure of an outline. They may choose to expand their summary or make a list of events. Whichever method you choose is fine as long as it gives you a place to work from. Let's stick to the outline for now, since it's got a solid structure.

Let's envision our story taking place in scenes or acts, like the action in a play or movie. It'll make it easier to visualize it. There are three scenes. Each is represented by a roman numeral. The details within the scene are noted by capital letters. Here's our outline:

STORY OUTLINE

SAMPLE STORY

I. **Sandy gets ready for school**

    A. She wakes up, gets dressed

    B. She eats breakfast

    C. She leaves her apartment

II. **Sandy arrives at school**

    A. She doesn't remember what room she is supposed to report to

    B. She goes to the main office to get help

III. **Sandy enters the classroom**

    A. She meets her first class

    B. She introduces herself as their new teacher

Okay. We've got our main character, our setting, and our plot worked out. And note that we've added another minor character—the person in the office that tells her which room to go to. We've got the bare bones of our story. In **Chapter 3: Writing the First Draft**, we'll put some flesh on those bones!

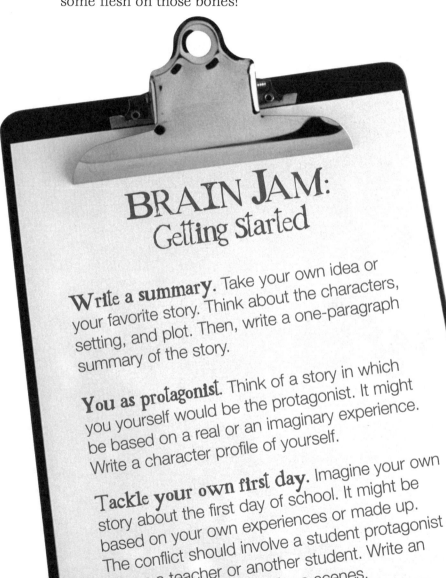

BRAIN JAM:
Getting Started

Write a summary. Take your own idea or your favorite story. Think about the characters, setting, and plot. Then, write a one-paragraph summary of the story.

You as protagonist. Think of a story in which you yourself would be the protagonist. It might be based on a real or an imaginary experience. Write a character profile of yourself.

Tackle your own first day. Imagine your own story about the first day of school. It might be based on your own experiences or made up. The conflict should involve a student protagonist versus a teacher or another student. Write an outline for your story in three scenes.

The job of ... tell the sto...
...art of the story

As you write, be awar...
have a beginning, a ...

A go...
and ...

Wrapping it up

Forget about spe...
and punctuation...

THINK OUT OF THE BOX

Writing the First Draft

Writing the First Draft

If you've plotted out your story in an outline, now it's time to start writing. Don't worry about it. Even the most experienced writers sometimes have a hard time getting started. But at least you shouldn't be suffering from a writer's greatest dread, writer's block. That's when you don't know what to write next. You at least have somewhere to start, thanks to your outline.

Your first version of your story is a first draft. The most important thing you need to accomplish in your first draft is telling your story. Get it down on paper from beginning to end. Forget about grammar, spelling, logic, and descriptive details. You'll have plenty of time to go fix all that later.

"I get writer's block a lot. Usually I just try to get through it—to write anything, because I know I'm going to do four or five drafts of a book."
— Louis Sachar (1954–)

As you write, you should be aware of your story's structure. Every story has a beginning or opening, a middle, and an ending.

Story Structure:

- **The opening** introduces the setting, the central character(s), and the conflict.

- **The middle** develops the character and moves the conflict forward by describing events in the plot.

- **The ending** brings the conflict to a climax and resolves it, ending the story.

The Opening:
Getting Off to a Good Start

A good story opening does more than simply introduce the characters and conflict; it also grabs the reader's attention and makes him or her want to keep reading to see what happens next. There are a number of ways you can craft an opening. But a **key thing to remember is to get right into the action**. Don't bore your reader with a long description of the setting or detailed information about your main character. Don't tell what's going to happen, show it happening. You can get into a character's background and other necessary information a little later. The first order of business is to set the stage dramatically for your story.

The Opening

Here is a first draft of the opening of our sample story.

THE OPENING

SAMPLE STORY

Sandy heard the alarm clock go off. She lifted her head from the pillow and shut it off. Then she remembered what today was. It was her first day at her new school, and she had never felt worse in her life.

In four short sentences, we have:

- introduced the central character

- set up the conflict

- captured the reader's attention

He or she will want to read on to find out what happens next, why the character is so apprehensive, and what will happen when she gets to school. Savvy writers that we are, we have not revealed that the character is an adult and a teacher. Based on the limited information given, it is safe to say that the reader will assume our heroine is a student.

KILLER Openings

Good short story writers often try to grab their readers by the throat with their opening sentences. How do these extraordinary openings compare with the ones we created on the left?

ORDINARY	EXTRAORDINARY
"Robert Suarez got a small part in the sixth-grade school play."	"In the school play at the end of his sixth-grade year, all Robert Suarez had to remember to say was, 'Nothing's wrong, I can see,' to a pioneer woman, who was really Belinda Lopez." —*Gary Soto, "The School Play"*
"One day Troy found something strange on the sidewalk."	"The tooth was lying on the sidewalk, camouflaged against the erratic pattern of embedded oyster shells." —*Patricia Windsor, "Teeth"*
"Howard Lindsey Townsend III was middle-aged and tired."	"Howard Lindsey Townsend III had reached the point in his life where things were not going to get any better." —*Steven Otfinoski, "The Appreciation Society"*
"I decided to build a Time Machine, although I'm not sure why."	"You do not build a Time Machine unless you know where you are going." —*Ray Bradbury, "Quid Pro Quo"*

The Middle:
The Heart of Your Story

The middle, or body, of your story keeps the plot moving forward, develops your characters, and shows them interacting with other characters. If you picture your story as a deli sandwich, the beginning and ending would be the two pieces of bread, and the middle would be the meat in between. It also charts the conflict as it moves toward its final resolution. It's important that as you write the body, you don't digress from the central conflict and the main character. Don't get sidetracked with flowery descriptions of settings, minor characters, and dialogue that aren't pertinent to the central conflict. On the other hand, don't rush through a key moment or skip over a shift in the plot.

TIP FILE

We said it before, but it's worth repeating. Don't be a slave to your outline! As you write, new ideas and thoughts will come to you. That's part of the creative process. If you get a new idea that isn't in your outline, go with it. The outline is merely a framework and should remain a flexible one.

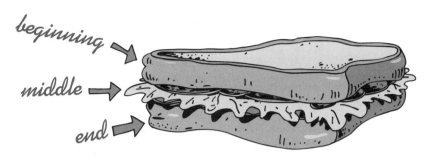

beginning →
middle →
end →

Here is a first draft of the middle of our sample story.

THE MIDDLE

She stood looking down the long corridor as questions ran through her head. Would the kids accept her? Would she fit in?

She tried to put such thoughts out of her mind. Suddenly, she couldn't remember the number of the room she was to report to. Sandy ran into the main office, where a lady looked up her name and told her the room number. She thanked the woman and walked quickly down the long hall, checking the room numbers as she went. She finally found the correct room and put a shaky hand on the doorknob. "This is it. Showtime," she said under her breath as she entered the room.

The Ending:
Wrapping Up Your Story

Your ending can be the most critical part of your story. It brings the conflict to a satisfying resolution for your reader. Just because the conflict is resolved doesn't mean that you have to tie everything up neatly with a ribbon. Some of the best story endings leave part of the action to the reader's imagination.

Let's turn to the ending of our sample story. Here are the last two paragraphs of the story. Sandy Anders enters her classroom with trepidation. It is a moment she has been dreading since the first line of the story.

TIP FILE

Keep writing! Poe said that ideally a short story should be read in one sitting. You might want to try and write your first draft in one sitting, too. That doesn't mean you can't stop to take a break, but if you can make it to the end of your story in one sitting, you can get a better grasp of the whole story and see more clearly which parts work and which don't.

THE ENDING

The classroom was filled with students who were talking and laughing. Some were sitting at their desks, and others were either standing or wandering around the cluttered room. The cacophony came to a sudden end and the room filled with an uneasy silence as they watched her make her way to the front of the classroom. Sandy swallowed hard and hoped no one could see her knees shaking.

"Good morning, class," she said weakly with a forced smile. "I'm Miss Anders, your new English teacher."

And there's our clever story's final twist.

The reader should be taken completely by surprise to find out that the new person at school is not a student but a teacher.

Don't Forget the Title!

Every story needs a title, and yours is no exception.
A good title whets your reader's interest and may reveal
something interesting about your story, its conflict and
characters. Depending on the kind of story you've written,
it can be mysterious, humorous, clever, or intriguing.

So what will we call our sample story? One thing a
title should not do is give away information that will spoil
the story for the reader. In the case of a story with a surprise ending, such as ours, this is particularly important.
So calling our story **"The New Teacher"** is definitely not
a good idea. You can't call it **"The New Student,"** either,
because this is deliberately misleading and untrue. A better title might be **"First Day."** It's descriptive but doesn't
give away the surprise. It's also short and catchy.

The Power of Potent Titles

Look at how a few changes can make an ordinary title
extraordinary. The extraordinary titles are from real stories
and are sure to excite readers' curiosity and grab their interest before they have read a word of the story.

ORDINARY	EXTRAORDINARY
"Shotgun's Last Night"	*"Shotgun Cheatham's Last Night Above Ground"* **Richard Peck**
"The Great Machine"	*"The Great Automatic Grammatisator"* **Roald Dahl**
"The Tomb"	*"There's a Tomb Waiting for You"* **Joan Lowery Nixon**
"Back to Life"	*"The Reincarnation of Sweet Lips"* **Larry Bograd**
"A Regular Day"	*"One Ordinary Day, With Peanuts"* **Shirley Jackson**

Put It Down!

Okay. You've persevered, kept writing, not worried about the details, and somehow finished your first draft. This is the time to put what you've written aside for a while. Stick it in a drawer for a day or two. You need some time to distance yourself from it. Then you can come back and look at it with fresh eyes and get on with the challenging work of revision. In **Chapter 4: Revising Your Way to Extraordinary**, we'll make some exciting revisions to our sample short story!

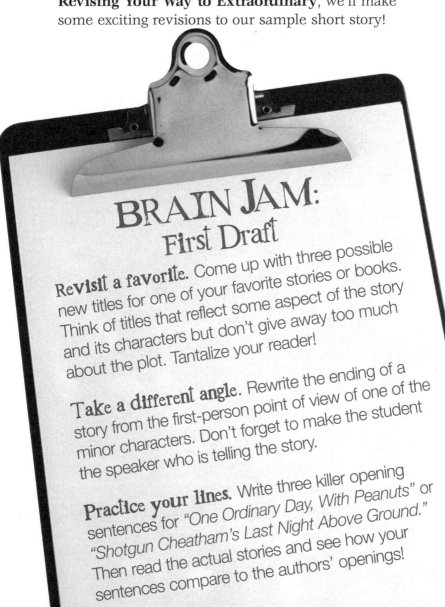

BRAIN JAM: First Draft

Revisit a favorite. Come up with three possible new titles for one of your favorite stories or books. Think of titles that reflect some aspect of the story and its characters but don't give away too much about the plot. Tantalize your reader!

Take a different angle. Rewrite the ending of a story from the first-person point of view of one of the minor characters. Don't forget to make the student the speaker who is telling the story.

Practice your lines. Write three killer opening sentences for "One Ordinary Day, With Peanuts" or "Shotgun Cheatham's Last Night Above Ground." Then read the actual stories and see how your sentences compare to the authors' openings!

A story's ending s
and should resolve

start in the middl

Revising is the
most challenging

se specific and colorful
ords and images.

THE SPIN ROOM

Revising Your Way to

EXTRAORDINARY

The Spin Room

"Good writing is rewriting," the writer and poet John Ciardi once said, and it's true. As you revise your draft, you'll start to look for ways to improve your story—tightening the plot, refining the conflict, developing the main character, adding or getting rid of a minor character or two.

THE OPENING

SAMPLE STORY

Sandy heard the alarm clock go off. She lifted her head from the pillow and shut it off. Then she remembered what today was. It was her first day at her new school, and she had never felt worse in her life.

Revising Your Opening

As you reread the opening paragraph of our sample you'll find that while it is okay, it isn't terribly interesting. Why not? Well, what's written describes the start of an ordinary day—ordinary in the sense that everyone gets up in the morning and goes to work or school. One way writers get their readers immediately involved in their stories is by starting in the middle of an action, not at the beginning. This plunges the reader right into the heart of the story. Let's say that instead of just waking up, Sandy Anders is already on her way to her first day at school.

Here's our original opening and a revised version of the same paragraph with this change.

THE REVISED OPENING

It seemed to take her forever to climb the tall steps leading up to Jefferson High and pass through the large wooden entrance doors. Sandy Anders's stomach was doing flip-flops. They started the moment she woke up an hour earlier and were still going strong. It was her first day at a new school, and she had never felt worse in her life.

We kept quite a bit of the original. But instead of waking up, Sandy is recalling that moment in the past. She is about to enter the school and face the challenge she dreads.

Revising Your Middle

As you revise the middle of your story, you will find some places where you need to cut and others where you need to add. It's all part of making your story the best it can be. Let's go back over those two sample paragraphs in the middle of our story and see where we can improve them. **Now, let's look at the changes to the text just as you might edit them on your first draft.**

THE MIDDLE

boring!

She stood looking down the ~~long~~ corridor as questions ran through her head. Would the kids accept her? Would she fit in?

She tried to put such thoughts out of her mind. Suddenly, she couldn't remember the number of the room she was to report to. Sandy ran into the main office, where a lady looked up her name and told her the room number. She thanked the woman and walked quickly down the long hall, checking the room numbers as she went. She finally found the correct room and put a shaky hand on the doorknob. "This is it. Showtime," she said as she entered the room.

make more dramatic

Note to Self:
Story needs more drama, stronger action verbs, and punchy descriptions.

THE REVISED MIDDLE

better adjective

empty

She stood looking down the ~~long~~ corridor as   **simile**

questions ran through her head *like a swarm of*

angry bees. ~~Would the kids accept her? Would~~

~~she fit in?~~ *Would she open her mouth and say*   **increasing Sandy's fears and our understanding**

something stupid that would make the class laugh

at her? It had happend before.

phrase intensifies Sandy's anxiety

She tried to put such thoughts out of her

mind. Suddenly *to her horror,* she couldn't

gives clear description of minor character

remember the number of the room she was to

darted   **stronger action verb**

report to. Sandy ~~ran~~ into the main office, where

a *pleasant* lady *with bright red hair* looked up

tells how she feels

her name and told her the room number.

Feeling foolish, she thanked the woman and

walked quickly down the long hall, checking

the room numbers as she went. She finally   **good dramatic touch**

found the correct room *and took a deep breath.*

She could feel her heart beating ~~fast~~ *like a tom-*

tom and put a shaky hand on the doorknob.

descriptive details heightens the drama of the moment

another simile

"This is it. Showtime," she said under her

breath *as she twisted the knob with trembling*

fingers and entered the room.

61

THE MIDDLE CLEANED UP

She stood staring down the empty corridor as questions flew through her head like a swarm of angry bees. Would the kids accept her? Would she fit in? Would she open her mouth and say something stupid that would make the entire class laugh at her? It had happened before.

Suddenly, to her horror, she couldn't remember the number of the room she was to report to! Sandy darted into the main office where a pleasnt lady with bright red hair looked up her name and told her the room number. Feeling foolish, she thanked the woman and darted down the long hall, checking the room numbers as she went. She finally found the correct room and took a deep breath. She could feel her heart beating like a tom-tom. "This is it. Showtime," she said under her breath as she twisted the doorknob with trembling fingers and entered the room.

We've made our story stronger and the character and her plight more engaging, with new word choices in our revision.

HOW TO ENLIVEN YOUR WRITING

Examples from Our Sample Story

Get specific. The more you work at making a character or object unique, the more that character or object will stand out for your reader. For example, the lady in the office is a very minor character who appears only for a moment, but we need to see her as a real person. She isn't simply a lady, but a "pleasant" lady. The "bright red hair" describes her physically.

Use good action verbs. Choose verbs that are exciting and colorful. Instead of saying Sandy "ran quickly," we substituted the stronger verb "darted." It creates a much more vivid picture of what Sandy is doing. Go through your story sentence by sentence and look for places where you can enliven the writing with strong, active verbs.

Add adjectives. Good adjectives bring people, animals, and things to life. They help create a visual portrait that readers can picture in their heads. It makes the person or thing specific, unique, and interesting. For example, the corridor being "long" is descriptive, but this doesn't say much more. By making the corridor "empty" we heighten Sandy's sense of being alone and indicate that she has arrived at school late.

Avoid adverbs. Adverbs modify verbs just as adjectives modify nouns. While adverbs like dangerously and anxiously can improve your writing, a reliance on adverbs can be a crutch for a writer. This is especially true when they are used to describe how someone said something. Example: "Stop that!" Jim shouted angrily. We already know from Jim's words and the verb "shouted" that he was angry. The adverb is unnecessary. Better to show Jim's anger through a visual image. Here's an example: "Stop that!" Jim said through gritted teeth. The effect is the same, but we get a visual image that sticks in our mind and shows us how Jim feels rather than tells us.

Use metaphors and similes occasionally. Similes and metaphors are comparisons of two unlike things. Similes use words such as "like" or "as" to link the two things. Metaphors are direct comparisons that do not use these linking words. By adding the simile "like a swarm of angry bees," Sandy's questions become truly menacing and destructive. When we say her heart is beating "like a tom-tom," you can hear the rapid beat and experience it emotionally. You don't want to sprinkle too many metaphors and similes throughout your story, but used sparingly, they can spruce up your writing and give your story a boost. 63

Here's our first-draft ending followed by a new ending that picks up where the old one left off.

THE ENDING

The classroom was filled with students who were talking and laughing. Some were sitting at their desks, and others were either standing or wandering around the cluttered room. The cacophony came to a sudden end, and the room filled with an uneasy silence as the students watched her make her way to the front of the classroom. Sandy swallowed hard and hoped no one could see her knees shaking.

lack of dialogue

"Good morning, class," she said weakly with a forced smile. "I'm Ms. Anders, your new English teacher."

ends abruptly

Revisiting Your Ending

The first draft of the sample story ends abruptly and doesn't give a satisfying resolution to Sandy's conflict. The closing surprise twist is nice, but it doesn't round out the story or give it a satisfactory ending. We've grown to identify with Sandy Anders and empathize with her insecurities. Her conflict needs to be resolved in some positive way. Anything less would be a downer for the reader.

Here's a new ending that's much, much better. What revisions did we make?

THE FINAL ENDING

SAMPLE STORY

"Good morning, class," she said weakly with a forced smile. "I'm Ms. Anders, your new English teacher."

A pimple-faced boy in the front row laughed, and then several other students giggled. It was already starting, she thought to herself. Just like at the last school.

descriptive detail

"Excuse me, ma'am," said a girl in the front row. "But you don't teach us English. This is home-room."

Of course the girl was right, and Sandy Anders laughed. The students laughed, too, but she could tell that most of them were laughing with her now, not at her.

"Thanks for the correction," she said. "You see, this is my first day here, and I've got some things to learn about your school. I'm hoping you can help me. Maybe we can help each other."

The students were smiling at her now. They liked her—for the moment, at least. It filled her with confidence. Maybe it was going to be all right after all, she decided, as she picked up the green attendance sheet from the desk and started to call out their names.

satisfying ending— doesn't end "life goes on"

descriptive details heightens the drama of the moment

The End

65

Sample Story: A New Ending

This ending of our sample story is infinitely better. It's positive, but not sugar-coated. Sandy will undoubtedly face more challenges as her first day continues, but she knows now that she is capable of handling whatever happens.

Another good thing about this ending is that it doesn't really "end." Life goes on as Sandy calls off the names of her students. If this story is supposed to be a realistic slice of life, this is a perfect way to show that life goes on beyond the story's ending.

How Many Drafts Are Enough?

You've finished your second draft. Should you do another draft? Probably. Maybe you'll need to write a third, fourth, or even a fifth draft. This doesn't mean you'll rewrite everything you've already written, but you might find small ways to improve your story. Remember, in a short story, every word counts! The more you work on your story, the better and more polished it will be. Only you know when it's ready to let go and show to another person—your first reader.

That first reader may have suggestions to make, too. If you respect this person's opinion, you should probably listen and make some or all the revisions he or she suggests.

While you refine your story, make sure you keep a dictionary and an English grammar and style book handy when you do your final draft. If you use a computer to write your story, it's okay to use the spelling checker, but don't rely on it. If you spell a word incorrectly but spell a different word, the checker won't catch it. You need to proofread your story yourself before printing out a final copy.

MAKING THE LAST DRAFT FINAL

No matter how many drafts you write, your last draft should be where you clean up all those little mistakes in mechanics and spelling that you've ignored until now. Here's a checklist to use as you go through your final draft.

✔ Is every word spelled correctly?

✔ Does every sentence start with a capital letter and end with a period, question mark, or exclamation point?

✔ Is the subject-verb agreement correct in every sentence?

✔ Proofread—ask someone else to read your last draft.

✔ Are there any grammatical mistakes?

✔ Have I included quotation marks around the dialogue?

✔ Have I numbered the pages of my story?

✔ Have I included the title at the beginning followed by my name as the author?

The EXTRAORDINARY Final Product

Okay. Our story is ready to be published. At about 470 words, it's considered a "short" short story. Now it's ready to share with others. So here it is, our sample story, finished and polished, and ready for the reading public. Read and enjoy.

THE FINAL PRODUCT

First Day
by Steven Otfinoski

It seemed like a short eternity before she finished climbing the massive concrete steps of Jefferson Memorial High and passed through the large, wooden entrance doors. Sandy Anders's stomach had been doing flip-flops from the moment she woke up an hour earlier, and they hadn't stopped. It was her first day at a new school, and she had never felt worse in her life.

Questions swirled through her head like a swarm of angry bees. Would the kids accept her? Would she fit in? Would she open her mouth and say something stupid that would make the entire class laugh at her? It had happened before.

She tried to put such thoughts out of her mind as she stared down the empty corridor. Suddenly, to her horror, she couldn't remember the number of the room she was to report to. Sandy darted into the office where a pleasant lady with bright red hair looked up her name and told her the room number. Feeling foolish, Sandy thanked her and hurried down the long hall, checking the room numbers as she went. She finally found the room and took a deep breath. She could feel her heart beating like a tom-tom in her chest. "This is it. Showtime," she said under her breath as she twisted the doorknob with trembling fingers and entered the room.

The classroom was filled with students who were talking and laughing. Some were sitting at their desks, and others were either standing or wandering around the room. The cacophony came to a sudden end, and the room filled with an uneasy silence as they watched her make her way to the front of the classroom. She swallowed hard and hoped no one could see her knees shaking.

"Good morning, class," she said weakly, with a forced smile. "I'm Ms. Anders, your new English teacher."

A pimple-faced boy in the front row laughed, and then several other students giggled. It was already starting, she thought to herself. Just like at the last school.

"Excuse me, ma'am," said a girl in the front row. "But you don't teach us English. This is homeroom."

Of course, the girl was right, and Sandy Anders laughed. The students laughed, too, but she could tell that most of them were laughing with her now, not at her.

"Thanks for the correction," she said. "You see, this is my first day here, and I've got some things to learn about your school. I'm hoping you can help me. Maybe we can help each other."

The students were smiling at her now. They liked her—for the moment, at least. It filled her with confidence. Maybe it was going to be all right after all, she decided, as she picked up the green attendance sheet from the desk and started to call out their names.

The End

Different Kinds of Stories

"First Day" is what is called a realistic story. It is set in the present. The characters are real, identifiable people. Many of the stories you read are realistic stories. But there are other kinds of stories, too, and they can be just as much fun to read and write. In the remaining chapters of this book, we're going to take a closer look at four kinds of stories—humorous stories, mystery and suspense stories, science fiction and fantasy stories, and historical stories set in the past.

STORY JUMP START

Now that you've seen how to write a story, here are a few suggestions if you are ready to get started on one of your own.

★ **Try a different point of view.** Pick a favorite story and try telling it from the point of view of a different character, such as the villain. For example, the book and Broadway musical **Wicked** explore the life of the Wicked Witch of the West from **The Wizard of Oz.**

★ **Tap your memory bank.** Take a vivid memory—for example, your most embarrassing moment, the arrival of your younger brother or sister, or your first day at a new school—and write a short story about it. Begin your story at the end.

★ **From today's headlines.** Lots of interesting stories can be found on the evening news, daily newspaper, or online. Pick one of the figures in the news and write a story about what happens next or what happened before.

EXTRA HELP

There are tons of style guides and dictionaries to choose from.

- ***The American Heritage Student Dictionary***

- **The Modern Language Association** (MLA) publishes a style manual that is often used when writing research papers.

- Take a look at ***The Elements of Style*** by William Strunk Jr. and E. B. White.

- If you find yourself getting stuck overusing certain words, visit the pages of ***Roget's Thesaurus*** or ***Scholastic Student Thesaurus.*** Watch your step, though. Don't go for words that you wouldn't be comfortable using in class. A word that's "too fancy" will appear forced in your story.

BRAIN JAM:
Experimenting With Words

Learn from the pros. Go through a favorite story and made a list of words, phrases, and images. Include action verbs, specific nouns, adjectives, and adverbs.

Start in the middle. Write an opening paragraph for a story about someone your own age facing a challenge from nature. It might be a rainstorm, an earthquake, or some other force of nature. Make your opening begin with an ongoing action.

Jazz up the ordinary. Write a description of someone doing something mundane—washing a car, shopping at the market, etc. Then go back and add stronger verbs and colorful adjectives to make the ordinary seem extraordinary. Add one metaphor or simile to your description.

ffbeat characters

An en

A clever parody

silly misunderstan

hat gets out of hand

AN Outrageous Predica

stories writ

WRITING THE HUMOROUS STORY

"Tragedy Is Easy, Comedy Is Hard."

Writing the Humorous Story

Everyone enjoys a good laugh. We watch sitcoms and stand-up comedians on television. We go to see our favorite comic actors in movies. We enjoy listening to and telling funny stories and jokes. Humor is an important ingredient in all kinds of literature, including stories, novels, and plays. Writers use humor to lighten up drama and provide moments of relief in mysteries and even tales of horror.

You might think writing funny stories is as easy as telling a joke. It's not. As one comic once said, "Tragedy is easy, comedy is hard." This may be an over simplification, but comic writers work very hard to tickle their readers' funny bones.

What Makes a Funny Story Funny?

Humor in fiction is quite different from the humor you hear from a stand-up comic. Humorous stories rarely rely on jokes or the kind of physical comedy you see in many films. As a short story writer you should look for humor in situations and characters. This kind of humor comes out of real life, not jokes. It's humor that we can identify with. That's what makes it not only funny but memorable.

Borrowing from Ancient Greek Comedies

There are some basic plots or situations that humor writers have been using since the days of ancient Greek comedies. Here are a few of them:

* **Mistaken identity** or other misunderstandings. Example: Your slightly scatterbrained Mother is expecting the plumber to come to fix a leak. Instead, a local politician running for reelection comes to call, and she mistakes him for the plumber. Wanting to get her vote, he attempts to solve her problem.

* **A predicament.** Example: You ask a girl you like to the school dance. She can't go. You ask another girl, and she says yes. Meanwhile, the first girl calls you back and says she can go after all. You really would rather take her, but you can't just dump your other date. So now you have two dates for the dance. How are you going to get yourself out of this mess?

* **An eccentric character** enters the picture. Example: Your uncle George comes for a visit. He likes to practice playing his trumpet at three o'clock in the morning. So much for getting sleep at your house!

As you probably have figured out already, the humor in these stories comes from the situations and characters. The wrong assumptions that come out of a misunderstanding, the way a character tries to extricate himself from a predicament, or the difficulties that arise from an encounter with an eccentric character all hold great potential for humor.

Memorable Voices from Funny Stories

The voice of a first-person narrator can be particularly important in a humorous story. The humor arises not only from the story itself but from the unique and colorful way in which the narrator tells it. The storyteller's point of view, or "spin" on the story, in which he or she played a part, adds to the humor, making it even funnier and more memorable. Here are four examples from the opening paragraphs of some published stories. The first one shows how an ordinary opening can become extraordinary when it has a voice:

ORDINARY

"Bill Driscoll and his partner Sam were in Alabama when they decided to kidnap the son of a well-to-do family and hold him for ransom. It turned out to be a bad idea."

EXTRAORDINARY

"It looked like a good thing: but wait till I tell you. We were down South, in Alabama—Bill Driscoll and myself—when this kidnapping idea struck us. It was, as Bill afterward expressed it, 'during a moment of temporary mental apparition,' but we didn't find that out till later."

—*O Henry,*
"The Ransom of Red Chief"

"Anyway, Mrs. Tibbetts comes into the room for second period, so we all see she's still in school. She's pregnant, and the smart money says she'll make it to Easter. After that we'll have a sub teaching us. Not that we're too particular about who's up there at the front of the room, not in this class."

—Richard Peck, "I Go Along"

"Mother says that when I start talking I never know when to stop. But I tell her the only time I get a chance is when she ain't around, so I have to make the most of it."

—Ring Lardner, "The Golden Honeymoon"

"Don't get the idea I'm a regular class cheat. It's true that if the kid sitting next to me during a test happens to be a genius and has his test paper out in full view of half the class, I'm not going to look the other way. I mean, I'm not stupid."

—Steven Otfinoski, "The Foolproof Plan"

"Humor is emotional chaos remembered in tranquility."
—James Thurber
(1894–1961)

Revisiting Our Sample Story: A Humorous Twist

Humor can be injected into any kind of story. For example, Sandy Anders's error in mistaking her homeroom class for an English class is a perfect case of humor that comes out of a misunderstanding. Let's go back and ask ourselves some "What would happen if . . ." questions in order to turn this realistic story into a funny one.

What would happen if...

… Sandy walked into the wrong classroom and found herself teaching English in a Spanish class? (misunderstanding)

… Sandy hadn't gotten much sleep the night before and had to struggle to stay awake on her first day at school? (predicament)

… Sandy's new principal pays a visit to her classroom, and he's a complete neat freak? (eccentric character)

TIP FILE

Reserve the humor in your story for your readers. Don't let your characters in on the joke. The more harrowing the problem they face and the more seriously they take it, the funnier the story. A surefire way to make your story un-funny is to let the characters see the humor in their situation for themselves!

Parody: Having Fun at Someone Else's Expense

A parody is a humorous imitation of something serious. It could be a book, a play, a movie, a television show, or even a song. The parodist follows the original in style but at the same time makes fun of it by using exaggeration and other humor techniques. You've probably read or seen and enjoyed numerous parodies. They are a staple of comedy shows such as **Saturday Night Live** and humor magazines such as **Mad**. A few years ago, a best-selling children's book was **The True Story of the Three Little Pigs.** This parody of the old folktale presented the Wolf as a misunderstood innocent (by his account) and the three pigs as responsible for their own downfall.

You can have fun writing about and parodying established characters from literature and popular culture. What's fun about this kind of humorous story is that you don't have to create a new character, only draw on the characteristics of the character that your readers will already be familiar with. By placing these characters in new and different situations, you can use your imagination to write a very funny story.

Here are some examples, again using our tried and true "What would happen if. . . " question format:

What would happen if...

... Snow White meets the Three Bears instead of the Seven Dwarfs?

... Dr. Frankenstein decided to create a dog in his laboratory as a companion for his Monster?

... Kyle, Stan, and Cartman from "*South Park*" ended up in Springfield with "*The Simpsons*"?

As you can see, the comic possibilities in such story ideas are endless. Predicaments, misunderstandings, parodies ... writing humorous stories can be a barrel of laughs!

HUMOROUS STORIES WORTH READING

"The Celebrated Jumping Frog of Calaveras County"
by Mark Twain

"The Secret Life of Walter Mitty"
by James Thurber

"Priscilla and the Wimps"
by Richard Peck

"Who Needs an Aries Ape?"
by Walter Dean Myers

STORY JUMP START

Revisit your worst nightmare. Almost everyone has a day when nothing goes right. Start with one of yours and see what you can add to make the story even more crazy.

Go extreme. Take the point of view of an animal or an inanimate object in a story. For example, a dog discussing a trip to the veterinarian's office.

Try your hand at parody. Try emulating a famous author's style in a type of story he or she would never write or writing a very serious story about something ridiculous.

BRAIN JAM:
Writing the Humorous Story

Think character. Come up with three story ideas based on two contrasting characters from fairy tales, movies, or television. Think about what you know about their characters and behavior. What funny possibilities arise from putting them together in a story? Write a scene from your story, but not the opening or ending.

Look for trouble. Think of a sticky predicament you once found yourself in that has comic possibilities. Write a one-paragraph summary of the situation that could be developed into a story.

Know anyone unusual? Who is the most unforgettable, unusual character you have ever met? Write a character profile of this person.

A puzzlin

Solid but perplexing c

Intriguing sus

satisfactory and

real motives

**WRITING THE MYSTERY
AND SUSPENSE STORY**

"It Was a Dark and Stormy Night"

"It was a dark and stormy night..."

A dark and stormy night is the perfect setting for a story full of mystery and suspense. But such stories can take place in almost any setting, including a green meadow on a bright, sunny afternoon. There are always dark shadows lurking in the corners, even on the sunniest days. You just have to look for them!

Mystery stories and suspense stories are often lumped together, but they are actually two quite different kinds of fiction. The mystery writer **Carolyn Wheat** compares a mystery to a walk through a fun house and a suspense story to a ride on a roller coaster. Both are apt comparisons.

"Over the crashing of thunder, he could hear a faint tapping against the window. . ."

Mystery vs. Suspense: What's the Difference?

Fun houses distort reality and creates illusions—so do mysteries. It is up to the character investigating the mystery to see through the illusions and find the solution to the puzzle.

Roller coasters offer wild and heart-stopping rides—so do suspense stories. They can take a character from the height of excitement one moment to the depths of dark fear the next.

When you read a suspense story, your emotions are manipulated as much as when you experience the twists and turns of a roller-coaster ride. There may be no mystery to solve, but there are plenty of thrills and chills to get through.

There are other important differences. In a mystery, the reader and often the main character, are in the dark, trying to figure out the solution. In a suspense thriller, the reader, but not the characters, knows all too well what is going to happen next or what might happen. The tension builds as that moment draws closer and closer.

TIP FILE

With mysteries, it's important stay focused on the plot. The mystery is more important than the characters or other story elements. Developing the characters too much would only detract from the mystery.

The filmmaker Alfred Hitchcock was known as the master of suspense because you usually saw the danger coming in his classic films. Mystery was often involved in his movies, but it never overwhelmed the suspense. Hitchcock himself once gave a good illustration of mystery versus suspense. A bomb has been planted under a table. In a suspense story, the reader knows the bomb's going to go off in ten minutes. The people sitting around the table are completely unaware of its presence. They sit there talking away about nothing in particular, but as the minutes tick away, the suspense grows greater and greater for the reader until it's almost unbearable. In a mystery, the bomb just goes off without anyone knowing it is going to happen. The rest of the story is taken up with someone trying to find out who planted the bomb and why.

Now let's look more closely at some of the important elements of the mystery story.

TIP FILE

Keep your story simple. Mystery novels have plenty of room for complicated plots. Mystery stories don't. Limit yourself to a few clues, a few suspects, and a clear and straightforward solution.

Revisiting our Sample Story:
A Mystery Unfolds

Let's go back to our sample story and see if, by adding a few new elements, we can turn it into a puzzling mystery. Let's get started with some "What would happen if . . . " questions and see where they lead.

What would happen if...

... Sandy Anders found her attendance book missing from her desk and suspected that one of her students had taken it? But which one and why?

... Sandy is happily surprised by an admiring note and an apple that were on her desk her first day? Each day she finds a new note and an apple on her desk. Who is her secret admirer, and what is he or she up to?

You can see from this last story idea that the mystery doesn't have to involve a crime, but could be something positive. It just has to be a mystery.

For the past five days, the raven outside Franklin's window watched his every move.

Clues, Suspects, and Red Herrings: Elements of the Mystery Story

To be a mystery, a story must have, well, a mystery. It could be an unexplained happening, an unsolved crime, or some other mysterious event. If it's a crime, it can be anything from a minor theft to a murder. Someone in the story sets out to solve the mystery. He or she could be a real detective (police or private) or an amateur detective who just stumbled onto the mystery.

The detective (let's call the character that for want of a better name) looks for clues, material things that will help to solve the mystery. A clue could be a fingerprint, an incriminating note, a footprint, or a thread of clothing left at the scene by the guilty party.

"… The tension is not the bodies in the snow and it is not the bodies in the closet, the body in the car trunk; the tension is the character of the person who wants to know the truth."
— Martin Cruz Smith (1942–)

The suspects are the characters in the story who could have committed the crime or act. In a mystery novel, there may be half a dozen or more suspects, but in a mystery story, there's usually room for only a few. As the detective gathers clues and puts together the information, he or she begins to eliminate suspects from the list and zero in on the culprit. In a good mystery, the reader is always a few steps behind the detective. He or she doesn't guess the real solution before the detective reveals it. If the reader can figure it all out before the ending, it's not a very good mystery.

Red herrings are suspects who are meant to seem guilty but turn out to be innocent. A brooding butler, a suspicious-looking friend, and a greedy relative with a motive for the crime all make great red herrings. Just remember that mystery writers have used red herrings for a long time, so you'll want to be careful that your reader doesn't have too easy a time spotting them. Use them sparingly.

TIP FILE

Keep it logical. It's good if your reader is pleasantly surprised by the outcome, but he or she shouldn't be mystified by it. Plan out your solution in advance, and make the clues believable but not too easy to figure out. There shouldn't be any loose strings left untied at the end that will make your reader feel confused or cheated.

Riding the Roller Coaster: Writing the Suspense Story

In a suspense story the focus is not on whodunit, but might be on how he or she is going to get away with it. Or the big question might be how the central character, our hero or heroine, is going to survive the dangers ahead. Here are some examples of opening scenarios for suspense stories:

You're camping in the desert with a friend. You wake up in the middle of the night to find a rattlesnake poised on top of your sleeping bag. It looks ready to strike. Trying not to move a muscle, you call out to your friend, who's sound asleep.

You happen, by complete accident, upon the answer key to an upcoming math test. You think about using it to ace the test, but resist. You just want to get it back to the teacher. But you know if he sees you returning it, he'll assume that you are a cheater. How are you going to get the answer key back to the teacher without getting caught?

TIP FILE

A good suspense story keeps the suspense building to an often-stunning climax. There's not much room to admire the scenery or get distracted by anything else but the driving force of the main action.

Revisiting our Sample Story: A Roller Coaster of Suspense

Our sample story already has a high degree of suspense built into it as Sandy Anders anxiously looks forward to her first day at school. But with some tweaking, we can ratchet up the suspense level even higher.

Mystery and suspense stories can be the most challenging to write. But the satisfaction you get when the story succeeds is immense. By controlling every twist and turn in your story, you can have the reader in the palm of your hand. You can make his heart beat faster with just a sentence, or make her gasp with surprise at your ending.

What would happen if...

> ... Sandy's new principal has told her that he is going to come in to observe her class in half an hour. The students are noisy and hard to handle. How will she ever get them under control before the principal arrives?

To make the suspense believable, it has to be plausible. The closer the situation is to real life, the more disturbing it will be for your reader. If your reader can identify with your main character as an ordinary person, he or she will keep thinking, "This could be happening to me!"

Memorable Dialogue from Extraordinary Mystery and Suspense Stories

Dialogue is important in all stories, but especially in mystery or suspense stories. Whether a detective is questioning a suspect or explaining a crime's solution, dialogue plays a key role in moving the plot forward. In a suspense tale, dialogue can dramatize the conflict between protagonist and the antagonist while revealing the personalities of the good guy and bad guy.

Here are examples from two truly riveting stories:

EXTRAORDINARY MYSTERY AND SUSPENSE STORIES

"Good morning, madam," said Holmes cheerily. "My name is Sherlock Holmes. This is my intimate friend and associate, Dr. Watson, before whom you can speak as freely as before myself. Ha, I am glad to see that Mrs. Hudson has had the good sense to light the fire. Pray draw up to it, and I shall order you a cup of hot coffee, for I observe that you are shivering."

"It is not cold which makes me shiver," said the woman in a low voice, changing her seat as requested.

"What then?"

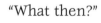

"It is fear, Mr. Holmes. It is terror."

—*Sir Arthur Conan Doyle,*
"The Adventure of the
Speckled Band"

".... You strike lighter successfully ten times running and Cadillac is yours. You like to have dis Cadillac, yes?"

"Sure, I'd like to have a Cadillac." The boy was still grinning.

"All right. Fine. We make a bet and I put up my Cadillac."

"And what do I put up?"...

"Some small ting you can afford to give away, and if you did happen to lose it you would not feel too bad. Right?"

"Such as what?"

"Such as, perhaps, de little finger of your left hand."

"My what!" The boy stopped grinning.

—*Roald Dahl,*
"Man from the South"

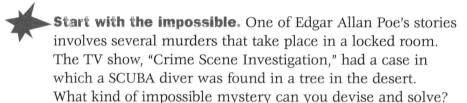

STORY JUMP START

★ **Think of being in a tight spot.**
It might be being trapped in an elevator or hanging for dear life from a mountain cliff. Write your suspenseful story from the point of view of the poor person experiencing it. Include no other characters. The protagonist is on his or her own in getting safely out of the predicament.

★ **Start with the impossible.** One of Edgar Allan Poe's stories involves several murders that take place in a locked room. The TV show, "Crime Scene Investigation," had a case in which a SCUBA diver was found in a tree in the desert. What kind of impossible mystery can you devise and solve?

★ **Make a discovery.** Many characters in mysteries and suspense stories get the action going by finding something accidentally. It could be a suitcase, a notebook, a series of numbers scratched on a window pane.

MYSTERY STORIES WORTH READING

"The Murders in the Rue Morgue" by Edgar Allan Poe

"The Adventure of the Speckled Band"
(a Sherlock Holmes mystery) by Sir Arthur Conan Doyle

"Miss Hinch" by Henry Sydnor Harrison

"Witness for the Prosecution" by Agatha Christie

SUSPENSE STORIES WORTH READING

"The Monkey's Paw" by W. W. Jacobs

"The Most Dangerous Game" by Richard Connell

"Man from the South" by Roald Dahl

"Sometimes They Bite" by Lawrence Block

BRAIN JAM:
Creating Mysteries and Suspenseful Elements

Set the scene. Imagine that you are the first person to arrive at a crime scene, overhear part of an evil plan, or witness a person being chased. Write an opening paragraph for your mystery story that brings the reader right into the initial crime or mystery.

Talk tough. Think up three suspense stories of your own. Write a tense, suspenseful scene between two characters—two friends, two enemies, two strangers, or even two enemies who pretend to be friends.

Believable chara

A plot that involv
or technology in

An imaginative s

A fantas

CHAPTER 7

FRANKLIN WATTS

WRITING THE SCIENCE FICTION AND FANTASY STORY

A Race of Superior Aliens Has Infiltrated Earth!

A Race of Superior Aliens Has Infiltrated Earth and...

SCENARIO 1

...is poised to launch an invasion. Only one young boy knows this terrible truth, but no one will believe him.

SCENARIO 2

...a team of scientists from the future travels back in time to prevent the assassination of a world leader and change the course of history.

SCENARIO 3

...an astronaut travels to the outer reaches of space to find a new home for the people of his dying planet.

If these three scenarios sound vaguely familiar, they should. **They are examples of three of the most durable themes in sci-fi: alien invasions, time travel, and space travel.**

SCI-FI STORIES WORTH READING

"2001" by Arthur C. Clarke

"There Will Come Soft Rains" by Ray Bradbury

"The Feeling of Power" by Isaac Asimov

"The Ones Who Walk Away From Omelas" by Ursula K. Le Guin

Welcome to the Imaginative, Exciting World of Science Fiction!

What exactly is science fiction and why is it so popular? **Science fiction is a kind of imaginative literature that draws its inspiration from science and technology.** Science fiction is often set in the future, but it doesn't have to be. It's often based on scientific fact, but it doesn't have to be. Science fiction can be deadly serious or a little silly. It can be about little green men from outer space. Or it can deal with the human race facing such challenges as war, political tyranny, or environmental pollution in the future. The only limits on science fiction are the borders of the human imagination.

Science Fiction vs. Fantasy—What's the Difference?

These two genres of story writing are linked, but just like mystery and suspense, they are distinct. **Science fiction deals with the possible or what could be possible**. Its power is derived from science and technology. **Fantasy deals with the impossible—that which could never be.** Its power is derived from magic and the supernatural. Science fiction is often set in the future. Fantasy often takes place in the distant past of myths and legends. The *Star Wars* films are science fiction. *The Lord of the Rings* trilogy is fantasy. Which is not to say that elements of science fiction can't be present in fantasy and elements of fantasy, can't be present in science fiction, but they're still separate and distinct and you should know this before attempting to write a story in either genre.

Dreams Grounded in Reality

Both sci-fi and fantasy are the most imaginative kinds of stories you can write. But here's the interesting part. To succeed as stories, the imaginative world the writer creates has to be grounded in some kind of reality. No matter how fantastic the events are in the story, the characters, whether human or nonhuman, have to be characters that we, as readers, can identify with. They have to have hopes, dreams, and lives that somehow parallel our own. Otherwise, there is nothing for the reader to care about and no one to root for.

Equally important, the reality the writer creates in a story, no matter how strange and unearthly, must have some kind of logic and consistency to it. When this occurs, the fantasy becomes all the more real and believable. If there's no logic, and no rules in this new world, the reader will quickly lose interest in it. This holds true whether the story is set in the future or on a distant planet.

"A [good] science fiction story is a story built around human beings, with a human problem, and a human solution, which would not have happened at all without its scientific content."

—Theodore Sturgeon (1918–1985)

Let's look back at the three sci-fi scenarios on page 100 and apply this principle.

SCENARIO

1 The space aliens are superior to humans in every way, but they are not invincible. Like the space invaders in **H. G. Wells's "The War of the Worlds,"** they are susceptible to earthly germs. In the end, the microbes destroy them before they can destroy the human race.

SCENARIO

2 The scientists have mastered time travel, but there are rules to time travel that they learn they cannot break. If they tamper with the past, they will change their present and cause untold damage to the future. Therefore, in the end, they reluctantly allow the assassination to take place and let events take their natural course.

SCENARIO

3 The astronaut must put himself in suspended animation during the long flight to the new planet to prevent his body from aging. When he returns to Earth, he finds that all the people he knew, including his family, are old or dead. He must face the colonization mission with a new generation of people he does not know. This creates problems for him.

We've given the scientific foundation behind all three of these stories. If you can include some science in the story you write, you will make it stronger and more interesting to your reader. But that doesn't mean you have to, and **Ray Bradbury,** perhaps the most popular living author of science fiction, often doesn't draw much on science in his stories. This has led some critics to call him a fantasy writer. Actually, Bradbury is an incredibly versatile writer who has written stories in a number of genres—science fiction, fantasy, suspense, mystery, horror, and even realism.

Memorable Sensory Descriptions from EXtraordinary Science Fiction and Fantasy Stories

Good short story writers paint vivid pictures in words that their readers can visualize in their minds. Sensory description includes words and images that relate to one of the five senses (taste, touch, smell, hearing, and seeing). Good sensory descriptions are particularly important in sci-fi and fantasy because they make the imaginary worlds the writer creates more real for the reader. Here are three excerpts from sci-fi stories that do this. As you read, see if you can pick out what sense each detail appeals to. In the first exmaple, we've again compared the ordinary to the extraordinary.

ORDINARY

"In one corner of the room was a container of Martian glass that was the brightest blue. Beck picked it up and set it down on a table … Sunlight passed through a side window and made the blue bottle even bluer than before."

EXTRAORDINARY

"It was there, in one corner of the room, a container of Martian glass as blue as the sky, the size of a small fruit, light and airy in Beck's hand as he set it down upon a table…. Sunlight spearing through a side window struck blue flashes off the slender container. It was the blue of a star held in the hand. It was the blue of a shallow ocean bay at noon. It was the blue of a diamond at morning."

—*Ray Bradbury,*
"The Blue Bottle"

MORE EXTRAORDINARY DESCRIPTIONS

"Marvin liked it here: it was fun watching the great, slender plants creeping with almost visible eagerness toward the sunlight as it filtered down through the plastic domes to meet them. The smell of life was everywhere, wakening inexpressible longings in his heart: no longer was he breathing the dry, cool air of the residential levels, purged of all smells but the faint tang of ozone."

— *Arthur C. Clarke, "If I Forget Thee, Oh Earth ..."*

"The sound of Gwilan's harp was water running and rain and sunlight on the water, waves breaking and the foam on the brown sands, forests, the leaves and branches of the forest and the shining eyes of gods and stags among the leaves when the wind blows in the valleys. It was all that and none of that."

—*Ursula K. Le Guin, "Gwilan's Harp"*

Frank was not prepared for this head-crushing and stomach-stomping plummet toward the earth.

Sample Story: A Real Sci-Fi Adventure!

Let's return once again to our sample story and see if some new "What would happen if ..." questions stimulate our imagination.

What would happen if...

... Sandy Anders's first day was at an interplanetary school where students came from all over the Milky Way?

... Sandy Anders discovers to her shock that some of her students are aliens sent to Earth on an exploratory mission?

... Sandy comes to the frightening realization that all the other teachers at her new school are robots?

STORY JUMP START

Look at life on another planet. Picture an earthling landing on another planet and confronting a technologically advanced civilization. Write about an encounter between the earthling and a reprsentative alien in dialogue, with a minimum of narration and description.

Get lost in space. Imagine being on a futuristic space vehicle when disaster strikes. The crew loses control over the vehicle. How does the crew react? What happens with the vehicle?

Go high-tech. Write a story around a new technology that radically changes some aspect of daily life. For example, e-mail changed the speed at which many people communicate. Remember to think about both the positive and negative results of this new technology.

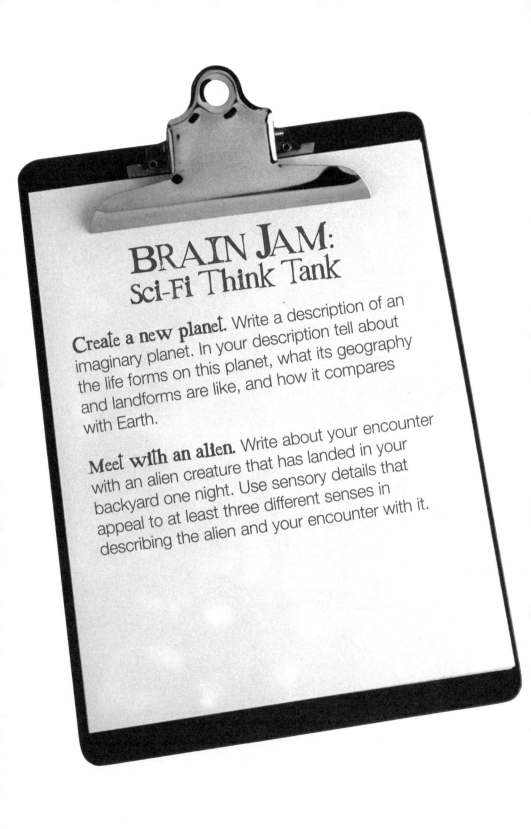

BRAIN JAM:
Sci-Fi Think Tank

Create a new planet. Write a description of an imaginary planet. In your description tell about the life forms on this planet, what its geography and landforms are like, and how it compares with Earth.

Meet with an alien. Write about your encounter with an alien creature that has landed in your backyard one night. Use sensory details that appeal to at least three different senses in describing the alien and your encounter with it.

ringing the past to

A conflict that comes ou
of your story

istorical details
ime period and b

Ficti

WRITING THE
HISTORICAL STORY

History
Doesn't
Have to be
Boring!

History Doesn't Have to be Boring!

Well, history doesn't have to be boring. After all, it is people who make history, and people are always interesting. The story of humankind is filled with exciting stories, fascinating people, and unforgettable events. And you have 5,000 years of civilization to draw on. That's a lot of potential story ideas to choose from.

Factual Events, Fictional Characters

Historical fiction includes any story set in the past. The story itself and the characters in it can be completely fictional, but the setting, or the time and place, must be real and historically accurate. Why not use real historical characters like George Washington, Daniel Boone, or Abraham Lincoln in your stories? You could. The problem is that when you use real people, you have to be careful what you say about them. You want to stay true to history and who that person was. The use of real historical figures can limit you in many ways, especially when it comes to developing your plot and conflict. Fictional characters give you much more freedom and don't present as many problems with accuracy.

Many writers of historical fiction use historical figures as minor characters in their stories. You might consider doing the same. These famous people can add a sense of authenticity to your story.

Story Ideas:
Melding Fact and Fiction

Where do you get an idea for a historical story? Because history is so vast a subject, and it's easy to lose your way, a good place to start might be with a specific historical event. This will help you develop not only your characters but also your conflict, setting, and plot. Let's take three events from U.S. history and see what story ideas we can develop from them.

EVENT 1 **Battle of Lexington** The battle between the British and the patriots at Lexington, Massachusetts, in April 1775 that sparked the American Revolution

EVENT 2 **Oregon Trail** The long and difficult journey of pioneers heading west along the Oregon Trail in the 1840s

EVENT 3 **Blizzard of 1888** The blizzard of 1888 that struck in March and paralyzed the Eastern seaboard, particularly New York City

All of these events are dramatic and could lend themselves to great stories, filled with action and adventure. Of course, you'll need a protagonist for each. Because you are a young person, you might choose someone your own age to be the protagonist. This way, you can put yourself in this person's position and experience the same things he or she is experiencing.

Story Ideas Based On Historical Events

Here are three story ideas based on story events featured on page 111.

EVENT

1 **Battle of Lexington A young boy accompanies his father to Lexington Green to face the British soldiers.** When the boy's father is wounded, the boy takes up his father's musket and fights in his place. The British move on, and the young man drags his wounded father to safety. He now feels part of the fight for freedom and is ready to join the cause in the coming war for independence.

EVENT

2 **Oregon Trail A family is traveling west with a covered wagon along the Oregon Trail.** They come to a raging river and must decide to cross there despite the danger or find another spot where the water isn't so high and fast-moving. They decide to face the challenge at this point rather than lose precious time going further downriver. The crossing is dangerous and they almost lose the wagon, but they finally make it safely across, ready to continue on their long trek.

EVENT

3 **Blizzard of 1888 A young girl lives in New York City in the 1880s with her father.** One snowy March morning, he goes off to work. As the day progresses, the snow continues to fall heavily, and the girl begins to worry about her father's safety. She goes downtown as the blizzard reaches its peak to find him. She has some hair-raising adventures before she locates her father, and the two of them return home safely.

Note that in each of these story ideas the conflict comes directly out of the historical event—a Revolutionary skirmish, a westward trek, and a terrible snowstorm. The protagonist in each case is a minor player in the greater event. Yet these protagonists are the main focus of the story. The plots are straight-forward with few surprises, but there is plenty of suspense, action, and adventure. Because the characters could be real people with feelings, desires, and fears, we care about what happens to them.

The events in the first and last event story ideas are self-contained and help shape the plots. You couldn't write a story about the boy as he went through the eight years of the revolution. That would take a novel to cover convincingly. By the same token, you couldn't show the progress of a dozen New Yorkers trying to survive the blizzard of 1888. That would take a novel, too. Focusing on one character's plight works perfectly for a short story.

The second event story, set on the Oregon Trail, isn't built around a single event. The long journey was filled with many challenges and dangers. But we have chosen one challenge to focus on in our story—the fording of a river.

"Stories are relics, part of an undiscovered pre-existing world. The writer's job is to use the tools in his or her toolbox to get as much of each one out of the ground intact as possible."
— Stephen King (1947–)

The Role of Research

Research for a short story? You might say, "I do research for reports in science and social studies, but not for a story. Stories come out of my imagination. I don't need research for that." This may be true in the case of many stories, but not historical ones. While your characters may be fictional, the world they live in is a very real one from a different time. It is your job as the story writer to make that distant world come alive for your readers. The only way to do this is to learn as much as you can about the period or event and include convincing historical details in your story. Use encyclopedias, history books, and other references works to find out how people at this time lived—what they did for a living, what kind of clothes they wore, and even what they ate. These details will enrich the background of your story, give it color, and hold your readers' interest. They'll be learning something while being entertained.

If your story revolves around a specific historical event, as in the case of our three sample story ideas, you'll want to research that event, too. Here are some questions you'll want to find answers for as you do your research:

EVENT

1 **The Lexington story.** What were the British doing at Lexington? What did the green where the fighting took place look like? What kinds of weapons did the British have? How did the patriots defend themselves? What were the casualties (dead and wounded) on each side?

EVENT

2 **The Oregon Trail story.** What did the covered wagons that the pioneers traveled with look like? What things did they hold? What other dangers did people traveling the trail face? What roles did women and children play on the journey?

EVENT

3 **The Blizzard of 1888 story.** Why did so many people go to work that fateful March day knowing a snowstorm was in progress? What dangers did the blizzard present to people of New York City? How many people perished in the storm in New York? What means did people use to survive the snow and the cold? What individual stories have been passed down about survivors and victims of this terrible natural disaster?

Memorable Settings from Extraordinary Historical Stories

A sense of place and time is critical to the success of a story set in the past. Here are three more passages from writers who re-create the past with wonderful descriptions of their settings.

ORDINARY

"We walked to the Fair that afternoon. The pavilions were huge and there were hundreds of people. There were too many people. They made me nervous.

Then we saw the giant Ferris wheel invented by George Washington Gale Ferris. It was the largest amusement ride I ever saw. Mama didn't want to go on it, but I did."

EXTRAORDINARY

"We walked to the Fair .... Once again I'd have turned back if Mama said to. It wasn't the awful grandeur of the pavilions .... It was all those people .... They scared me at first, then .... My eyes began to drink deep ....

There it rose before us, two hundred and fifty feet high. It was the giant wheel, the invention of George Washington Gale Ferris. A great wheel with thirty-six cars on it, each holding sixty people. It turned as we watched, and people were getting on and off like it was nothing to them.

'No power on earth would get me up in that thing,' Mama murmured."

— *Richard Peck,*
"The Electric Summer"

MORE EXTRAORDINARY DESCRIPTIONS

"Annie stood shivering by the railing of the boat. Looming ahead, standing majestically in the center of the harbor, was the shape of a gigantic lady holding a torch in one hand and a tablet in the other.

'You believe it, too, Annie,' she could almost hear Geoffrey saying. 'The Statue of Liberty will be here in New York Harbor—the entire lady, lighting the harbor and welcoming ships and people from all over the world.' Tears filled Annie's eyes. She was suddenly glad she had come."
— *Pam Conrad, "A Brother's Promise"*

"It was near sunset when Mike Braneen came onto the last pitch of the old wagon road which had led into Gold Rock from the east since the Comstock days. The road was just two ruts in the hard earth, with sagebrush growing between them, and was full of steep pitches and sharp turns. From the summit it descended even more steeply into Gold Rock in a series of short switchbacks down the slope of the canyon. There was a paved highway on the other side of the pass now, but Mike never used that."
— *Walter van Tilburg Clark,*
"The Wind and the
Snow of Winter"

Revisiting Our Sample Story: A Trip Back in Time

Let's look at our sample story and see how we might transform it into historical fiction. Sandy Anders is a contemporary woman living today. But what if she lived a hundred years ago or more? Let's try another "what would happen if . . . " question to turn this contemporary, realistic story into a blast from the past:

What would happen if...

... Sandy Anders lived in the 1870s in the rural United States and her first day teaching in this community was spent in a one-room schoolhouse?

TIP FILE

Don't get so carried away with your research that you forget you're writing a story and not a history essay. Adding too many interesting facts and details will make your characters fade into the background when they should be standing out in the foreground. Use the historical past to strengthen your story, but never lose sight of your characters, their feelings, and the immediate conflict they struggle with.

Facing Facts

Obviously, you will want to do some research into one-room schoolhouses before you write a word of your story. Here are some interesting facts you learn that will help you write your story and develop your conflict:

- In the one-room schoolhouse, children of all ages were put together and the teacher's challenge was to meet all their needs as best she could.

- In cold weather, the teacher and students were responsible for keeping the wood-burning stove going to provide enough heat for the schoolhouse.

- The teacher had no principal or other authority figure to turn to for help. She was the sole authority and had to maintain discipline and order as best she could.

As you can see, each of these facts could be used to develop your story and its conflict. The facts you learn will stimulate your imagination and get your creative juices flowing. So turn back the pages of time and write a story that will make history come alive. There is nothing boring about that!

HISTORICAL STORIES WORTH READING

"The Death of Jack Hamilton" by Stephen King

"The Electric Summer" by Richard Peck

"A Brother's Promise" by Pam Conrad

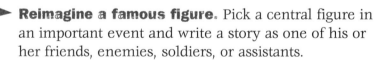

STORY JUMP START

⭐ **Start young.** Look back at a historical event you have studied in history class or one you recall from your own lifetime. Write a story about the event from the perspective of a young person such as yourself. Remember that the protagonist needs to face a conflict involving this event.

⭐ **Reimagine a famous figure.** Pick a central figure in an important event and write a story as one of his or her friends, enemies, soldiers, or assistants.

⭐ **Explore a difficult situation.** Tell the story of a person out of step with his or her environment. For example, a farmer during the Dust Bowl or a banker during the Great Depression.

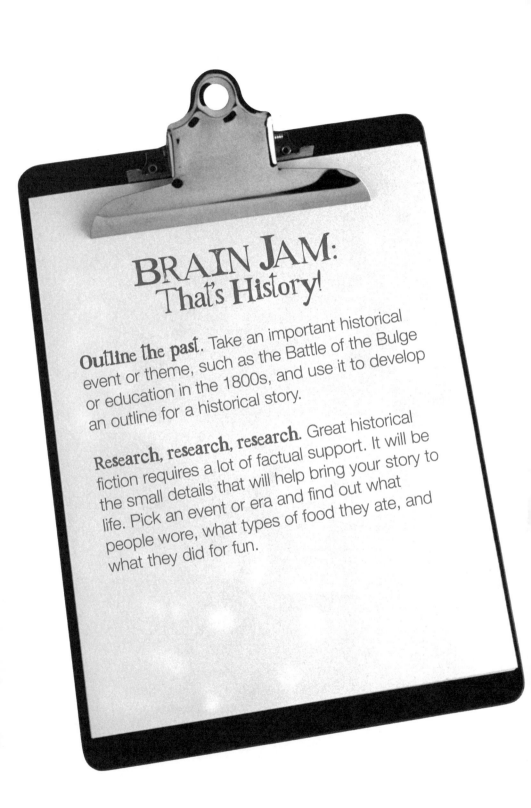

BRAIN JAM:
That's History!

Outline the past. Take an important historical event or theme, such as the Battle of the Bulge or education in the 1800s, and use it to develop an outline for a historical story.

Research, research, research. Great historical fiction requires a lot of factual support. It will be the small details that will help bring your story to life. Pick an event or era and find out what people wore, what types of food they ate, and what they did for fun.

TO FIND OUT MORE

Books

Baechtel, Mark. *Shaping the Story: A Step-by-Step Guide to Writing Short Fiction*. New York: PearsonLongman, 2004.

DeMarinis, Rick. *The Art & Craft of the Short Story*. Cincinnati, OH: Story Press, 2000.

King, Stephen. *On Writing: A Memoir of the Craft*. New York: Scribner, 2000.

Knight, Damon. *Creating Short Fiction: The Classic Guide to Writing Short Fiction*. New York: St. Martin's Griffin, 1997.

Lucke, Margaret. *Schaum's Quick Guide to Writing Great Short Stories*. New York: McGraw-Hill, 1999.

Phillips, Kathleen C. *How to Write a Story*. New York: Franklin Watts, 1995.

Sheriff, John Paxton. *Practical Short Story Writing*. Victoria, BC, Canada: Robert Hale & Company, 1999.

Sizoo, Bob. *Teaching Powerful Writing: 25 Short Read-Aloud Stories with Lessons That Motivate Students to Use Literary Elements in Their Writing*. New York: Scholastic, 2001.

Sorenson, Sharon. *How to Write Short Stories*. Lawrenceville: NJ: Thomson/ARCO, 2002.

Whiteley, Carol. *The Everything Creative Writing Book: All You Need to Know to Write a Novel, Short Story, Screenplay, Poems, or Article*. Avon, MA: Adams Media Corporation, 2002.

Organizations and Online Sites

Classic Short Stories
http://www.classicshorts.com

This site has more than one hundred classic short stories to read and learn from. A number of the stories given as resources in this book can be found here.

DynamicFiction.Net
http://www.dynamicfiction.net

This site includes book reviews of short stories, writing resources, and a chance to submit and get your short story "published" online.

Storymind.com
http://www.storymind.com

You'll find free articles, classes, and tips for writing fiction, plays, and screenplays on this site. It also sells writing software and other products.

Teen Ink
http://www.teenink.com

Written by teens, this monthly magazine publishes short stories, poetry, essays, and reviews. It also publishes a series of books of teen writings and post material by teens on its Web site.

Twenty Great American Short Stories
http://www.americanliterature.com/

Read stories by some of America's best short story writers, such as Edgar Allan Poe, Jack London, and Mark Twain.

Writers Digest
http://www.writersdigest.com

Maintained by Writers Digest, a leading national magazine for writers, this site includes information about Writers Digest annual writing competitions, which are open to young writers, and lists the 101 best Web sites for writers.

INDEX